Russell Westbrook

— — — — — ✎✎✎✎ — — — —

The incredible story of Russell Westbrook—one of basketball's greatest players!

or interim quality. Trademarks that mentioned are done without written consent and can in no way be considered an endorsement from the trademark holder.

Table of Contents

Introduction

Thank you for picking up this book, all about Russell Westbrook.

This book aims to serve as a biography of sorts, giving you an insight into the life and journey of the NBA superstar, Russell Westbrook.

You will soon learn about Westbrook's upbringing in a tough neighborhood, how he managed to overcome the odds, impress coaches, receive a College scholarship, and finally, make the NBA.

While his journey is far from over, it has been very exciting to watch Russell Westbrook dominate the court throughout his career. Currently, he's playing better than ever with a presumably long time left in the league.

This book details both Westbrook's biggest challenges and accomplishments, and concludes by speculating over what's next for Russell Westbrook, both off and on the court.

Thank you once again for taking the time to read this book, I hope you find it to be an insightful and enjoyable read.

Chapter 1:

The Early Life of Russell Westbrook III

Born on November 12, 1988, Westbrook is now just 28 years old at the time of writing. Most fans would consider this to be young Westbrook's early days, but he's packed a lot of living into such a short period. Long Beach, California was his birthplace, but his roots were in Hawthorne—on the cusp of the violent streets of South Central Los Angeles. One might think that's where Oklahoma City Thunder's basketball star got his fiery spirit and gritty determination, but his parents were too smart to allow Russell and his brother, Raynard, to run with the gang's in South Central.

Instead, his parents, Russell Sr. and Shannon Horton, led their boys to participate in the second most popular activity for young black men in South Central—basketball. With Dad's military field drills and practice play setups on the community courts, it was no accident that Westbrook would shift from playground king to one of NBA's most recognized and honored court leaders.

Not only was sports emphasized in the Westbrook home, but education was also high on their list of priorities. As a well-liked, honor roll student, basketball wasn't Russell's only option; it was his passion, and that's quite evident to all who watch him on the court. His speed, grace, and agility are just a few of the remarkable traits that attract the most loyal of fans. What endears him to us all? It is his genuine character and willingness to work harder and longer than almost any other star athlete. Does he have an ego? You bet he does, and he's earned every moment of fame.

It wasn't always fame and fortune for Westbrook. Growing up in a community where 75 percent of the young people dropped out of high school, and less than 10 percent of those who continued graduated from college was no easy feat. In such a diverse community, it wasn't unusual to see Latinos, Blacks, and Asians hanging together in the streets. Those living in and around South Central L.A. lived in a culture with the flavors, music, and traditions of the American melting pot. While outsiders see the mean streets of South Central L.A. as poverty stricken urban blight, Westbrook refers to it fondly as the place of his most remarkable childhood memories.

Most of Westbrook's days as a spindly-legged kid were spent sharing stories of school at the dinner table as he enjoyed his mother's cooking, and learning what it was to be a man from his dad's careful mentoring. If Russell and his brother were on the streets, it wasn't to raise havoc, but rather to learn how to be responsible and hard-working young men by the inspiring involvement of their parents. It was there that Russell dreamed of playing the game in front of millions. It was a distant dream, but he was more than willing to put in the work to make it a reality.

Walking into Leuzinger High School as a scrawny freshman, Westbrook wasn't drawing much of a crowd of admiring females or envious athletes. His 5'8" height wasn't going to guarantee him an NBA spot. In fact, it didn't even win him a spot on the basketball team's starting lineup. Other than his speed, he was easy to overlook. It appeared that all his father's insistence on daily pushups and sand sprints taught him nothing outside of self-discipline and determination. The question was, would that give him a winning ticket? Even in those early days, it wasn't enough for Westbrook to just be an average member of the team, he had to lead—to win—to lead the winners!

His coaches had to pay close attention to Westbrook to see past his minimum height to his size 13 feet. Therein lied the secret, Westbrook had a lot of growing to do to fill those shoes. However, Westbrook and his neighborhood friend, Khelcey Barrs, didn't let a little thing like awkwardness and uncontrolled aims kill their dreams of making it to the pros. Most conversations began and ended with them one-upping each other with stories of their athletic prowess and how others would envy them when the NBA recruited them. Not once did they envision the tragedy to come.

It was during their sophomore year that Khelcey was giving it his all in a pickup game. As far as anyone knew, 16-year-old, 6'6, 200-pound Khelcey hadn't been suffering the kind of discomfort that indicated a severe heart attack was on its way. Unfortunately, cardiac arrests don't always announce their arrival, and Khelcey's enlarged heart gave no warning. He collapsed during the game and was rushed to the hospital where he was later pronounced dead. Westbrook's life changed with the absence of his best friend, but his resolve to play pro grew even stronger.

Barrs had all the hopeful coaches in his back pocket when he led along the school team to win the 2003 Southern Section Quarterfinals. Now that Barrs was gone, they weren't exactly keen on shifting gears to give Westbrook a gander. Although Barr had received offers from coaches all over the country, Westbrook had only a few from Creighton, Loyola Marymount, and Kent State. Instead of giving up and letting Barrs down, Westbrook dug in and began playing ball with a passion that few had seen then or since. At only 15 years old, Westbrook learned that you need to make every day count because it could be your last.

The summer between Westbrook's sophomore and junior year was a game changer for him. He finally grew into those shoes, reaching his adult height of 6'2" tall and experiencing a weight gain of forty pounds. He was quicker on the courts than ever, and the combination was catching the attention of coaches from coast to coast. Knowing your life could be changed in an instant had somehow changed Westbrook, always stepping on the court like he had something to prove.

When UCLA's head basketball coach, Ben Howland, visited Leuzinger High School to see coach Reggie Morris, he wasn't all that gung-ho to see Westbrook, but when speaking to Coach Morrison the phone he promised Howland, he'd be pleased with the young player's zeal and talent. Of course, that was the mantra of most coaches he visited, but Howland kept an open mind. He knew Westbrook was quick on his feet, but it took more than that to become a member of one of the best college basketball teams in the country.

It was early morning, and nobody but the cleanup boy was in the gym. As he waited for Coach Morris to enter the gym, his mind was preoccupied with other things as he gazed at the young man pushing the broom back and forth on the basketball floor. His actions were precise, almost reverent, checking to make sure he hadn't missed a spot—giving each board his undivided attention.

Coach Morris finally entered with a smile and an offered hand. "So, where the kid? I thought he might be with you."

"He's right down there," he replied, pointing to the boy sweeping the gym floor. There was little that Howland saw during the game that day that impressed him as much as what he saw in Westbrook as he proudly did his job. Howland knew if Westbrook took that much care in a menial task, he would perform unbelievably in a game in which he felt deeply passionate.

After finishing his work, Westbrook went into the locker room and inspired the players to play like it was the state finals. Howland knew he had a tiger by the tail, a leader whose presence on UCLA's team could make all the difference. Like many other high school recruits, Westbrook was raw and unpolished, but played with recognizable potential. Although Howland recognized Westbrook's possibilities, he had no idea that he had just recruited a young man who would become one of the best NBA players of all time.

When you compare photos of Westbrook as a boy and Westbrook as a man, you'll see that same intense look, the same sharp features and determined stare, and the same proud countenance that are the makings of a leader. He doesn't play basketball; he feels its rhythm in sounds of the dribble, the cheers of the fans, and the silence as he holds his breath in wait of the receiving hoop. Just as he felt the game on the streets of South Central, he feels its calling in every arena in the nation. Just as he did as that somewhat awkward kid who went through the drills with his dad, he still goes through the motions that continue to make him great. He might not be sweeping the floor anymore, but he still takes great pride and pleasure in the little things that got him where he is today.

But, we get ahead of ourselves. Westbrook's next step was to decide what university to attend, with many anxiously awaiting his call. Where would be the best place to begin his career? In the end, it was the very school that he and his best friend had dreamed of for years. Now it would be up to him to carry on the dream, and Westbrook was determined to do Barr proud.

Chapter 2:

Westbrook's College Career

Westbrook didn't know it yet, but Ben Howland's visit was the precursor to what was to become a spectacular college basketball career at UCLA. Howland returned to UCLA to discuss Westbrook with Kerry Keating, who was UCLA's assistant coach and one of Westbrook's biggest fans. He looked at Keating with a doubtful expression on his face as he first spoke to Keating. "Well, he's not a point guard," Howland commented, trying unsuccessfully to play the devil's advocate.

Keating came back with a laugh, saying "Did I say he was a point guard? No, I just said the kid could play."

There was no disagreement with that statement, but they both knew Westbrook had a lot of work to do to become Bruin's material. UCLA's assistant, Donny Daniels, echoed their sentiments, but after seeing him play, Daniel's also recognized Westbrook's potential, and all began speculating the possibilities. It wasn't a stretch for them to know they could have a star on their hands. Sure, Westbrook made all the stupid mistakes of a young colt, with forced plays that didn't work, decisions that weren't any better than his forced plays, and a bevy of air balls that could have endangered high flying birds trapped in the gym.

Two things just couldn't be denied—his exceptional speed and the intensity in which he played that enabled him to dominate the court and lead his teammates to victory. He also had an unstoppable work ethic. Keating witnessed Westbrook's court magic six times during his senior year, which was all the NCAA would allow. Each time Keating watched a game, he made sure Russell Sr. saw how interested he was in his son's talent on the court. Howland sure didn't want another scout to come in a swoop Westbrook up before he could convince UCLA that this young kid was going to be their next man of the hour.

Westbrook wanted to get a basketball scholarship to UCLA, and there was no denying that Keating and Rowland thought he'd be a good catch, but there was a holdback. Jordan Farmar hadn't said for sure he was going pro, and if he decided to stay with the Bruins, that would push Westbrook out of contention. There just wouldn't be an opening for Westbrook's position. Howland was confident that Farmar would stay put, but Keating knew that Farmar's desire to turn pro was too much for him to resist.

It seems Keating was right, and Farmar's declaration to go pro left a spot for Westbrook. Although Arizona State was showing serious interest in Westbrook, he went with his and his best friend's dream—playing at UCLA. Westbrook signed his letter of intent at UCLA, and he wore the K3B band, taking Barrs with him in memory.

The transition from South Central Los Angeles to UCLA was not as difficult for Westbrook as many had imagined. Although he missed his family, he formed some close friends in the tight circle of basketball hopefuls. One of those basketball players who made his freshman year at UCLA better was Miss Nina Earl. Nina was a beautiful, female basketball player who shared his love for the game and soon shared her love for Westbrook, and he for her.

Westbrook's dedication to basketball didn't diminish the fact that he still wanted the full college experience. He had always made friends easily, and college life provided him with many opportunities to experience new things and make friends who are still important to him today. Baseball, football, and women's basketball were some of the things Westbrook enjoyed the most—well, those and hanging out with Nina. Westbrook's popularity was growing tremendously, on and off the court.

Westbrook was getting along well off the court, but on the court, he was floundering. His speed both pleased and frustrated the coaches. Although they were harsh on Westbrook, they were no harder on him than he was on himself. Picking Westbrook out on the court was easy. He was the one wearing the meanest scowl and maintaining the tensest posture when he made mistakes, which was much of the time. Turbo-charged Westbrook just didn't have any other gear but high, and when he was moving like a bat out of hell, others had no time to set up the play. Somehow, they had to find a way to slow him down. Consequently, much of his freshman year was spent trying to figure out how to master his control while flying down the court. However, playing only nine minutes per game didn't exactly provide the practice he needed to hone his skills, and his averages of 3.4 points and 0.7 assists did nothing to showcase his real talent.

That summer was a move-maker for Westbrook, as he dug in his heels and decided he was going to listen and learn to play big-league style. It wasn't unusual to see him every morning before dawn at the gym practicing his hoops and then following that up with a challenging workout with the weights to build his body and give him the strength he'd need to hold his own with the taller brutes who tried to run him down on the court. Most of the time they just couldn't catch him, but when they did he wanted to be prepared to fight back.

A champion of pickup games, Westbrook looked forward to testing himself against the visiting pros. He'd pit himself against Kobe Bryant, Carmelo Anthony, and Kevin Garnett, and his agility and speed often made them dread having to guard the little speed demon. After watching his progress that summer, Howland knew this was bound to be Westbrook's year to prove to everyone that he could hold his own with other top players all over the country.

The better Westbrook played, the more he played—and, the more he played, the better he got. It was a beautiful cycle, and he was taking every opportunity to create magic on the court. He was finally settling into his own, which was never more evident than when they played Michigan State. Westbrook controlled the court for 40 minutes with only one turnover. He had learned another thing this summer, and that was how to be aggressive without drawing the foul. The Pac-10's Player of the Year Defensively went to Westbrook, which was an outstanding reward for all his hard work.

Howland's year was going very well, and he was congratulating himself for his wise decision to sign Westbrook—until the season ended and Westbrook announced he wanted to go pro. Wanting to have more time to coach and mold Westbrook, Howland tried to discourage him, but Westbrook held firm to the idea of placing his name in the draft pool. Not only did Howland want to coach Westbrook, but he had to admit that Westbrook had turned into such a leader, the team would suffer at his loss.

After declaring for the draft, Westbrook didn't just sit back and wait for the draft. He had always had a curious mind, and he was more interested than ever how he could become the best player in the NBA. It never occurred to Westbrook that his name wouldn't make the draft, but he wasn't satisfied with just making the draft. Like everything else, he wanted to dominate the draft. The first round was the only place that was acceptable, and among the first five was his preference. Like everything else he did, he did it with confidence and a winning spirit.

Westbrook pestered his trainer, Rob McClanaghan, to meet him at Santa Monica High School almost every day for workouts that lasted an eternity. Westbrook wouldn't quit until his legs were shaking and his clothing soaked with the sweat of his resolve. The grittier the workout, the better he liked it. His body began to take on a harder exterior, and his mind formed more defined goals that helped him to slow down and control the play. Westbrook was determined to be ready for the draft and recognized for the player he could become if he had an opportunity to join the NBA.

Because of his speed, Westbrook's pull-up jump shot wasn't exactly pretty, to say the least. Like most other players whose focus is quickness on the court, Westbrook's challenge was with the pull-up jump shot. Much like how his father had done in his early childhood, McClanaghan worked him like a drill sergeant. He'd run him from one foul line to the other foul line, then make him pull up for the jump shot. It was grueling, but Westbrook worked and never complained, at least not in McClanaghan's earshot. He welcomed the full test of his endurance and played every practice as if it was for the championship.

When Russell Westbrook III was the 4th draft pick overall, some people thought he was the luckiest kid in the league. What they didn't realize was that luck had little to do with it. Westbrook had a plan, and he worked it to perfection. Only five rookies under twenty-one years old scored an average of 4 rebounds, 5 assists, and 15 points per game and Westbrook was one of them. The other four had been Magic Johnson, LeBron James, Chris Paul, and Allen Iverson, so Westbrook had aligned himself with the best of the best.

It wasn't luck that won Westbrook a high draft position; it was hard work. He was always the first to arrive at training and the last to leave. Westbrook made the most of every pickup game, every workout, every association who might be able to offer wisdom and new strategies. He avoided drama off court, but he welcomed it on the court, rarely willing to miss a chance to score even when he had to pit himself against players far bigger and brawnier than he was. He was the scrappy, aggressive, gritty boy from South Central Los Angeles, and he was about to make his debut on the courts of kings.

Howland was there to see Westbrook win a place with the Seattle Sonics. It was 2008, and Westbrook had come far from the playground star of South Central. His parents and brother were filled with pride as Westbrook was a first-round draft choice—first round—imagine that! Where was that skinny kid who couldn't get the attention of more than three colleges, now? Oh, there he was, looking at playing in the NBA at just 20 years old.

This time might have been the end of a long struggle for Westbrook, but it was the beginning of an incredible career.

Chapter 3:

On His Way to the NBA

Westbrook had two incredible seasons playing for the University of California at Los Angeles, leading the 2007 and 2008 teams to be one of the top four teams every year he attended. He was remembered by his teammates as much for his personality, encouragement, and leadership, as he was for his talent. Now he was starting over again, a little fish in the big Seattle SuperSonics' pond of players. Or so he thought! However, change is a frequent visitor to the NBA, and so the SuperSonics were about to discover. In 2008, on July 5th, Westbrook decided to join the Sonics. Technically, he never played for the SuperSonics because just after he got drafted, the team sold and moved to the mid-west to become the Thunder of Oklahoma City.

The summer that he should have been spending with coach Carlesimo preparing for his first season in the NBA was now going to be taken over by his replacement, coach Scott Brooks. Most of the team were taken aback by the news, but Westbrook's positive attitude and easy acceptance served him well once again. Just a few months after signing on as their newest rookie, Westbrook scored 10 assists, 17 points, and 10 rebounds to give him a triple-double.

Throughout his first season, he averaged 15.3 points, 5.3 assists, almost 2 steal per game, and just shy of five rebounds, earning him fourth in line for the title of Rookie of the Year. He lost to good company, holding his own to follow O. J. Mayo with the Memphis Grizzlies, Derrick Rose who won the title with the Chicago Bulls, and Brook Lopez who played for the New Jersey Nets at the time. He managed to make it onto the NBA All-Rookie First Team, and his family and Nina were cheering him on all the way.

The next season was better than the first for Westbrook, with his average continuing to rise to 16.1 points, 8.0 assists, 4.9 rebounds, and 1.3 steals. He once again moved his team to successfully battle the Timberwolves, scoring a personal career record of 16 assists and ten points. His teammates and coaches were thrilled to double their wins the second season Westbrook played, enabling his team to make the cut for the playoffs, carrying a 50-32 record. Even though they were eliminated in the first round, Westbrook played like a gladiator, averaging 20.5 points, a little over three steals per game, 6 rebounds, and 6 assists.

He continued to dominate the boards, and the fans went crazy in November of 2010 when he played the Pacers to score forty-three points, which topped his previous career-high. The next month he totaled nine assists, thirty-eight points, and a personal best of fifteen rebounds in a game that took Thunder and the Nets into triple overtime. His continued success didn't go unnoticed by almost every head coach of the NBA; consequently, they selected Westbrook to be an All-Star Game reserve player for 2011, in the Western Conference.

The Thunder had chosen a winner by the name of Westbrook, and they were joining him in the winner's circle. The season ended at 55-27, losing in the finals to the Mavericks. However,

Westbrook was still on the rise, averaging for the playoffs a little over six assists, 23.8 points, and just over 5 rebounds. He was on fire, and so were all the Thunder fans.

The 2011-12 season for Westbrook was an incredible repeat of the last, with the coaches voting to have him play in the All-Star Game for 2012. The season was cut short by the basketball lockout, but Westbrook still racked up the stats, averaging 23.6 points, 5.5 assists, 4.6 rebounds, and 1.7 steals for the season. This season Westbrook made All-NBA Second Team once again.

On June 12th, the first game of the finals, Westbrook posted 27 points and 11 assists, beating the Miami Heat 105-94. He joined an elite league with Michael Jordan as just two players to score ten plus assists and 25 plus points as they starred in their finals debuts. Once again voted an NBA All-Star player, he finished the 2012-13 season averaging 23.2 points, 7.4 assists, almost two steals, and over five rebounds per game. Westbrook was on a roll, and nothing could stop him as the Thunder gained the #1 position in their conference. Just about the time one thinks nothing is standing in the way of becoming champions, something does. That something was an injury to Westbrook's right knee. When stealing the ball from Westbrook, Rockets guard Patrick Beverley plowed into him hard. Westbrook was obviously hurt, but he continued to play. In fact, he had scored a whopping 29 points to end the game.

It was later discovered that Westbrook required surgery. For the rest of the playoffs, Westbrook was benched on the sidelines, licking his wounds, but he wouldn't be down for long. In fact, Westbrook was honored once again that year by being awarded the All-NBA Second Team for yet the third time. However, his knee continued to bother him, and just before the 2013-14 season, Westbrook underwent another knee surgery. Everybody predicted he'd be out for several games during the first part of the season, but in real Westbrook style, he missed just two games before returning. During Westbrook's injury, Kevin Durant continued to keep the Thunder competitive, and Westbrook played light for a while until his knee got stronger and more stable.

In the 2014 season, Westbrook was the alpha once again, leading his team to a 59-23 finish, earning them the second place in the Western Conference. In the fourth game of the finals, while playing the Spurs, Westbrook stole the ball five times, scored an incredible forty points, made ten assists, and rebounded five times. He now belongs to another elite club with Michael Jordan, being the only two players to post such remarkable scores during just one game of the playoffs. Although the Thunder did not win, Westbrook averaged an incredible seven rebounds and eight assists per game, while scoring twenty-six points or more. It was an outstanding season, and Westbrook and Durant had become the league's "golden" boys, with a pairing that was hard to beat.

The next season, the two of them weren't as fortunate. Both suffered injuries and were sidelined together, with Westbrook's fractured hand and Durant's broken foot. Their absences created a massive loss for the Thunder, and it was doubtful whether they would make the playoffs. Westbrook refused to be down for long, returning with 32 points scored in a game that gave them the winning score over the Knicks. The following game, Durant returned, and the two of them worked their court magic to lead the team to a seven-game winning streak and put them back into contention for the playoffs.

The month of February was a stellar month for Westbrook, with averages for each game of at least 10 assists, 31 points, and 9 rebounds. Westbrook would go on to nab an incredibly impressive three additional triple-doubles before the season came to an end. With a passion for making the playoffs, on April 12th, he scored 54 points, but it wasn't enough to push the Thunder to their goal. They finished a disappointing 9th in the West.

Much like Michael Jordan and Scottie Pippen did for the Bulls in the '90s, Westbrook and Durant did for the Thunder in 2015. Game after game they posted record scores, with Westbrook and Durant each scoring at least 40 points in just one game. Two players that put up 80 plus points—not much less than a whole team could score. They were making history and creating plays that were near impossible to defend.

On August 30, 2015, Westbrook experienced the highlight of his life—his marriage to Nina. They had a fairytale Beverly Hills wedding with all the trimmings. Westbrook never does anything second-class, and his wedding followed suit. Westbrook's love of the game doesn't foreshadow his love for family. In fact, he has an unusual ritual of calling his parents, wife, and brother before every game.

The year 2015 marked another score for the Westbrook family as their youngest son, Raynard, graduated from college. Nobody could have been prouder than brother Russell. When Raynard graduated, it was Westbrook that was there to hand him his diploma, smiling ear-to-ear. They had both achieved their dreams, and nobody worked more diligently than their parents to see to it that they did.

Westbrook was given almost $86 million for extended his contract with the Thunder for an additional three-years, and he earned every bit of it. Kevin Durant's departure to the Golden State Warriors hit Westbrook hard, but as always, Westbrook's positive attitude and "I can do it" determination continued to make him one of the highest scoring players of all times. He felt Durant's loss, but he had suffered worse losses and recovered to become a champion. He knew what it was like to pull himself up and let the game give him the courage to compete. Even though he had yet to win a Championship, he was what champions were made of, what coaches coveted, what fans admired, and what families respected.

You often see winners on the court, but their personal lives are not so remarkable, and many of them make the papers for entirely different reasons than being successful. Westbrook is one of those rare individuals whose personal life is a bigger win than anything he's achieved playing basketball. His relationships are steady, and his family is supportive, and those are the things that have made Westbrook a real winner. Westbrook's life has not always been whistles and bells, but the tragedies he has experienced has made him stronger and more determined to prevail over the hardships.

Unrelated to his scores on the court, Westbrook has the makings of a champion. He has the heart and courage of a leader who realizes to be a leader he first must serve. Westbrook serves his teammates each time he gets on the court, he serves as a role model for his brother and all the young men trying to find their way, and he serves as an iconic example of what caring and wise parents can instill in their children. All that is what makes for a winning Westbrook season!

Chapter 4:

Westbrook's Professional and Personal Challenges

You would think one of Westbrook's biggest challenges was making a success of his life when he was a product of the streets of South Central Los Angeles, but he doesn't look at things that way. What he remembers most about growing up in one of the roughest places in America is the love of dedicated parents and a brother who looked up to him. He remembers the tight-knit community, and his best friend who lived right across the street. Westbrook doesn't see his childhood as something he had to overcome; he sees it as an advantaged upbringing that provided him with the passion and work ethic to make him a success.

Though Westbrook doesn't spend a lot of time looking back; he's got his eyes focused on the present. However, there were quite a few challenges he had to overcome to get where he is today. Unfortunately, he loved a game that had a habit of favoring big, tall, brawny men, and Westbrook didn't fit the bill for many scouts and coaches. His 5'8" height and 140-pound build didn't qualify him as professional potential. Consequently, his high school years were spent trying to prove himself every time he went out on the court.

Some thought he had a chip on his shoulder, and perhaps his gritty, raw play was evidence of that. But it was that chip that gave him power, speed, and the "no mercy" attitude of a winner. Just looking at his early stats wasn't so impressive, but when coaches saw him play, they immediately recognized a star in the making. When necessary to make the point, Westbrook would dive for the floor to save a play and take a solid hit to set up a play for the team. With the odds against his ever playing in the NBA, Westbrook insisted on working toward that goal all the same.

One of the most challenging and life altering events in Westbrooks life was the sudden death of his best friend when he was just a sophomore in high school. It had a profound effect on his dedication to the game, but most of all on his insight into life. When you lose a friend who is that dear to you, and they leave your life so unexpectedly, every day becomes a gift. That's how Westbrook lives his life; as if it were a gift that is appreciated and paid forward.

Another significant loss in Westbrook's life was when Kevin Durant left the team to go play with the Golden State Warriors. They were such an incredible pair on the court that Westbrook believed he would enjoy their teamwork for the rest of his career. When Durant left the team, it was clear that Westbrook felt abandoned and betrayed. Westbrook took Durant's departure personally, and he wasn't shy about letting it show. Since then, whenever they have met on the courts, Westbrook wears his disappointment on his glaring expression and in the set of his body every time he goes head-to-head with his old teammate.

Like almost every NBA star, it's been a challenge for Westbrook to balance a personal life with his demanding career. When you are as dedicated to the game as Westbrook, the fans become your extended family, and you appreciate their support as you do your parents, sibling, wife, and close friends. He never minds signing an autograph or taking selfies with the public, but sometimes the demands made on a professional athlete can be taxing. It's always a balancing act between their family and career.

Westbrook's been fortunate in his career on the court not to be plagued by injuries, but all of that comes at a cost as well. When you're a bit smaller as a player, your body takes a beating. Westbrook works hard to make sure that he stays healthy and fit, ready to meet the physical challenges of the game as well as the emotional ones.

Because he's such an incredible athlete, his talents have also been a challenge for him to overcome at times—especially controlling his speed. Good team leaders are expected to set the game's tempo, and that means giving your team time to make the plays you've set up for them. This whole tempo thing was a difficult concept for Westbrook because he was such a gun and run player. Part of the problem was that nobody could match his speed, so there was little support for him at the end of the court. In the early days, his control was so erratic that he often lost the ball and experienced lots of turnovers. However, good coaching, lots of hard work, and maturity took care of his problem, and now he benefits from the speed he has learned to bridle.

Passion and pride are such a part of Westbrook that he has trouble not taking it personally when somebody scores against his defense. He can't sit on the sidelines and relax between plays because he's too involved with every play, directing every player as he shouts from the sidelines. When his teammates screw up, he's the first to let them know about it. However, he's also the first to congratulate them and encourage them when they work hard and do well. Watching Westbrook on the sidelines is like riding a roller-coaster of emotions. When he's on the up, everybody is enjoying the ride; when he's on the down, there's a sideline full of misery.

Some players fail under the unrealistic expectations of others, but not Westbrook. He exceeds expectations and sets a whole new standard for success. Just getting by would be considered failure for Westbrook whose vision has always been to win— and win BIG! He may not be big in stature compared to other NBA stars, but he's big in motivation, dedication, drive, passion, aggression, and leadership. He's big on putting forth everything and then some, giving the game 200 percent every night.

One of Westbrooks greatest career challenges is always to want to beat his best stats. When you're scoring, assisting, rebounding, and stealing as much as Westbrook, where is the ceiling? When will it occur to him that it's impossible to get much better than that? When will the bar get too high for him to hurdle? We thought we had seen it in his 2013-14 season after Westbrook suffered his knee injury that required not one but two surgeries, but that was not the case. His impatience and dedication didn't allow him to take off the three weeks as expected. Instead, Westbrook reluctantly laid out two games and then came back to lead his team to tally up win after win that next season. Did he suffer pain and make personal sacrifices? You bet he did, but that's how Westbrook rolls.

Westbrook was always the Thunder leader, but he also had Durant running right alongside him to make the plays and deflect a lot of the pressure. It's never been easy for Westbrook to trust, but he and Kevin had a professional trust that was unshakable. Now Westbrook needs to shift that to several others to complete the plays, and that's going to be his next big challenge. In the past, things got dicey when Westbrook would depend on his teammates, so he learned to handle most everything himself. Without Durant, Westbrook will need to rely on several teammates to pick up the slack, which will force them all to contribute to the good of the team. It will be interesting to see who will become Westbrook's new "go to" guy.

All the challenges of fatherhood will soon be coming Westbrook's way as well. With the birth of he and Nina's first child, Westbrook will be using that speed of his to keep up with his new baby. He is well-prepared with all the love and lessons he got from his parents, and Nina will be sure to give the child all the love and support she affords her husband as well. However, no matter how predictable and talented you are on the court, life has a way of interfering. Fatherhood, especially, will create for Westbrook a whole other adventure.

Since Westbrook is one to live in the present, he'll be sure to have his focus on this 2016-17 season. They have a grueling schedule and very fierce competition for the playoffs, but that's old hat for Westbrook. He thrives on rough schedules, gritty practices, and heavy travel. He welcomes working in the trenches and tends to create magic in the moments when his team needs him the most. He flourishes under pressure that would bury the average person and embraces the energy and excitement of every playoff game. Westbrook never fails to show up emotionally as well as physically, and his positive nature and endless energy have led his team to many of their challenges. He's used to people expecting his best, and he delivers.

You'll see him get angry and frustrated, but you'll never see Westbrook give up on the game. He hangs on to every play, milking every move for the most he can get. Westbrook doesn't hope the team wins; he expects the win. He accepts the attention he gets for winning and the criticism for every loss. He takes it personally when things don't turn out as he planned, and his plan is to win.

Some of Westbrook's challenges have yet to come, the greatest of which will most likely be when it's time to retire his jersey and make room for other hopefuls to play out their careers. At just 28, Westbrook isn't thinking of this, and who could blame him. When you're at the top of your game, all you can think of is staying there.

Chapter 5:

Westbrook's Most Notable Career Moments

The significant moments in Westbrook's career have been so many in number that they could make up an entire book in themselves, but we'll try to highlight some of his most outstanding achievements by year.

2006-07

- Recruited by UCLA Bruins

- 2006—Scored 14 Double-Doubles, 30 or More Points on Eight Different Occasions

- 2006—Recorded Career Best of 51 Points at Carson

- Earned Third-Team All-Conference Honors in Pac-10

- Senior Year—Averaged 25.1 Points, 8.7 Rebounds, 3.1 Steals, and 2.3 Assists

- Led team to a 25-4 Record His Senior Year

- Won this year's Defensive Player for the Pac-10

- 2008—Declared for the 2008 NBA Draft

2008

- Selected 4th Overall in the NBA Draft by Seattle SuperSonics

2009

- First Career Triple-Double with 17 Points, 10 Rebounds, and 10 Assists—Only Third Rookie In Thunder Franchise History to Make Triple-Double

- Averaged 15.3 Points, 5.3 Assists, 4.9 Rebounds, and 1.3 Steals for Season

- Finished Fourth in the 2008-09 Rookie of the Year

- Named to NBA's Rookie First Team

2010

- Averaged 16.1 Points, 8.0 Assists, 4.9 Rebounds, and 1.3 Steals for Season

- Recorded 10 Points and Career-High 16 Assists in an 116-108 Victory Over the Minnesota Timberwolves

- Took Team to Playoffs by Helping Thunder to Double Their Wins with a 50-32 Record

- In the Playoff Series, Westbrook averaged 20.5 Points, 6.0 Rebounds, 6.0 Assists, and 3.2 Steals

- Scored Career-High 43 Points against the Indiana Pacers

- Scored 38 points, 9 Assists, and New Career-High of 15 Rebounds in Triple-Overtime Win Over the New Jersey Nets

- Finished the Season averaging 21.9 Points, 8.2 Assists, 4.6 Rebounds, and 1.9 Steals

- Named to the All-NBA Second Team

- Took Team to the Western Conference Finals with the Dallas Mavericks

- Averaged 23.8 Points, 6.4 Assists, and 5.4 Rebounds in Playoffs

- Took Team to a Win for First World Championship Since 1994

2011-12

- Selected by NBA Head Coaches as a Reserve for the All-Stars

- Chosen by NBA Head Coaches to Participate in 2012 NBA All-Star Game.

- Scored Career-High 45 Points in Double Overtime Win Over Minnesota Timberwolves

- NBA Lockout—Still Averaged 23.6 Points, 5.5 Assists, 4.6 Rebounds, and 1.7 Steals for Season Cut Short

- Helped Lead Thunder to NBA Finals Once Again

- Game One of Finals He Recorded 27 Points, 11 Assists

- Joined Michael Jordan as Only Players with 25 Plus Points and 10 Plus Assists in NBA Finals Debuts

- In Game Four of Finals, Westbrook Had Career-High Score of 43 Points

- Finished 2012-13 Season Averaging 23.2 Points, 7.4 Assists, 5.2 Rebounds, and 1.8 Steals Per Game

- Won Second Gold Medal in 2012 Summer Olympics

2013-14

- Selected for NBA All-Star Game Once Again

- Lead Thunder to Playoffs #1 Seed in the Western Conference

- Suffered Injury to Right Knee—Still Scored 29 Points that Game

- Had Surgery—Out for Rest of Playoffs

- Named All-NBA Second Team for the Third Year

- Underwent 2nd Knee Surgery

- Recorded His Second Triple-Double of Season—13 Points, 14 Assists, and 10 Rebounds in Only 20 Minutes—2nd Fastest Triple-Double in NBA History

- Game Four of Western Conference Finals with San Antonio Spurs, he scored 40 Points, 5 Rebounds, 10 Assists, 7.3 Rebounds, and 5 Steals

- Became First Player Since Oscar Robertson in 1964 to Average 26 Points, 8 Assists, and 7 Rebounds in Playoffs

2015

- Scored 38 Points in Season Opener with Portland Trail Blazers

- Suffered a Fractured Right Hand

- Missed 14 Games

- First Game Back—Scored 32 Points

- Made His Ninth Career Triple-Double with 17 Points, 15 Rebounds, and a Career-High 17 Assists to Beat Golden State Warriors

- Fifth Player in NBA History to Record 15-15-15 in one game

- Scored Career-High 48 Points in One Game

- Played in All-Star game and 41 Points in Only One-Half

- Named All-Star MVP—Set All-Star Record for Scoring 27 Points in 11 Minutes

- Earned Third Triple-Double of Season and Eleventh of Career—Didn't Play the Fourth Quarter

- Scored 40 Points, 13 Rebounds, and 11 Assists—First Player with Three Straight Triple-Doubles since LeBron James in 2009

- The Month of February—Averaged 31.2 Points, 9.1 Rebounds, and 10.3 Assists Per Game

- Became First Player Since Michael Jordan to Have Four Consecutive Triple-Doubles and Back-to-Back Triple-Doubles with Scoring 40 Points

- Then Scored Fifth Triple-Double in Six Games

- Scored Seventh Triple-Double of the Season with 30 Points, 17 Assists, and 11 Rebounds

2015-16

- Opened Season with Game-High 33 Points and 10 Assists

- Westbrook and Durant—First Pair to Each Score 40 Points in Single Game Since Pippen and Jordan

- Scored 20th Career Triple-Double, with 22 Points, 11 Assists, and 11 Rebounds to Beat the Wizards

- Three Days Later—Second Straight Triple-Double with 21 Points, a Career-High 17 Rebounds, and 11 Assists to Beat Philadelphia 76ers

- Named Conference Co-Player for December Along with Durant

- Had 16 Points, 15 Assists, 8 Rebounds, and 5 Steals Against the Hornets—Fourth Player in NBA History with At Least 15 Points, 15 Assists, 5 Rebounds, and 5 Steals in One Game

- Third Straight Triple-Double and the Eighth of Season with 24 Points, a Career-High 19 Rebounds, and 14 Assists to Beat the Magic

- Voted to Start in His First All-Star Game

- Earned His Second MVP Aware

- Scored 31 Points, 8 Rebounds, 5 Assists, and 5 Steals in Just 22 Minutes—First Player in All-Star History to Win Consecutive MVPs

- Recorded His Eleventh Triple-Double of Season with 25 Points, a Career-High 20 Assists, and 11 Rebounds to Beat the Clippers

- Recorded His 15th Triple-Double of Season and 34th of Career with 21 Points, 15 Assists, and 13 Rebounds to Beat the Rockets

- Most Triple-Doubles by a Player in a Season Since Magic Johnson in 1988-89

- Sixth Triple-Double in March, which was the Most in one Month with the Exception of Michael Jordan Years Earlier

- Scored his 18th Triple-Double of the Season to Beat Los Angeles Lakers—Tying Magic Johnson for Most in a Single Season in the Past 50 Seasons

- Took the Thunder to the finals, Recording His Fifth Career Playoff Triple-Double with 36 Points, 11 Rebounds, and 11 Assists Only to Lose the Series to the Warriors

2016-17

- Signed a Whopping Three-Year, $85.7 Million Dollar Contract Extension with the Thunder—Third Highest-Paid Player in League

- Recorded His 38th Career Regular-Season Triple-Double with 51 Points, 13 Rebounds, and 10 Assists to Beat the Phoenix Suns—First 50-Point Triple-Double Since Kareem Abdul-Jabbar in 1975

- Recorded Seven Straight Triple-Doubles—Longest Triple-Double Streak Since Michael Jordan in 1989

- The Only Player to Average a Triple-Double for Entire Season

- Westbrook Joined Robertson and Chamberlain as Only Players in NBA History to Record 20 Triple-Doubles in a Season

- He Recorded 72th Career Triple-Doubles and 30 for Season—Passing Larry Birds Record

Basketball highlights for Westbrook occur in every game, scoring consecutive triple-doubles game after game. His achievements are remarkable, and his awards countless. Westbrook doesn't go into a competition wanting to break records, though. He goes to win and to beat his best. If the team is losing, he takes little pleasure in knowing that he reached a career-high in rebounds or assists. What's important to him is the win.

Many people would say that what's important isn't a win or a loss, but rather the pleasure which comes from playing the game. Westbrook doesn't subscribe to that kind of thinking. To him, it's all about how you play the game—and how he plays is to win. If Westbrook has a great game but the team is losing, that wasn't such a great game after all. If Westbrook gives it his all and it wasn't enough to win the game, he believes he didn't give it his all. Playing with that kind of intensity can be a challenge when you've broken as many records as Westbrook. You'd think there was nothing much left to play for, but not so for Westbrook. What's left to play for is a win for the next game. Yes, he's concerned about stats and records, but what drives him is his passion for winning. The only court battle he wants to participate in is the one where the team comes out with the win.

So, what's Westbrook's most notable career moment? The next one!

Chapter 6:

The Next Success Step for Russell Westbrook

It's hard to say what the next success for Westbrook will be because he's still right in the middle of his basketball stardom. When you're young and own the court, it's not like you're fixated on another career. The one remaining milestone that he is yet to achieve is the ultimate goal of winning an NBA championship. Currently, the Oklahoma City Thunder aren't considered a likely contender, despite Russell's best efforts. In the coming years however, it's quite possible that Westbrook will finally be able to tick this goal off of the list.

For a while, Westbrook's basketball career, his "Why Not? Foundation," his fashion line, and most of all his loving family and fans are more than enough to keep him busy. However, when the time comes for Westbrook to bow out of basketball, he probably won't be leaving the limelight.

With everything he's got going, there's an ocean of opportunity awaiting his attention, and Westbrook's drive and passion will push him to another star status in any endeavor he should choose. Let's look at what could capture more of his interest in the years to come.

WestbrookFrames.com

Cool is Westbrook's middle name when it comes to fashion and design, and it has never been more evident than in his lines of glasses frames. Their bold creations, crazy patterns and vibrant colors, along with their wide variety of shapes are taking frame designs to a whole new level. If you didn't need to wear glasses, you'd still be tempted to sport still the Westbrook look in a collection of stylish frames. They're not the most affordable, so save your cash for a quality frame, priced between $45 to $145 and up.

Clothing Line

Westbrook didn't stop with the frames, wanting to help you complement the new you with comfortable and stylish sportswear as well. From footwear to athletic attire and casual clothes for kids, Westbrook has developed that one-of-a-kind looks that allows you to express your independence confidently. He has designed clothing for everyone's tastes, from solid pastel pieces to exercise wear that is just a bit edgy. He's as proud of his clothing line as he is of his on-court achievements, which means you're going to pay the price to get that Westbrook look. So, be prepared to open your wallet along with your imagination. Whether you're conservative or crazy, it won't be hard to put together an outfit that has your name written all over it—literally!

The Why Not? Foundation

Westbrook's "Why Not? Foundation" was organized to give inner-city kids a sense of community, and to help underprivileged families find a way to promote pride and confidence in their children. They run events, such as the

"Why Not? Bowl" which is an annual event that helps fund community programs for at-risk youth.

Through this fundraiser and others that Westbrook's foundation sponsors, he has launched nine reading rooms in Los Angeles and Oklahoma City. Each reading room is equipped with 1,200 books for kindergarteners through to fifth graders. There are also stereo CD listening stations so kids can listen to their favorite artists without disrupting those reading. To encourage literacy and deliver the "escape through reading" message, they also have provided audio libraries with fluency CDs.

Because Westbrook wants to give back to those who supported him and help families place a higher value on education, he continues to provide access to thousands of books in reading rooms across the country. He works hard through book fairs, holiday dinners, and programs for homeless families to ensure they have opportunities to expand their minds.

One of his favorite foundation activities are the annual basketball camps. Not only are Westbrook and his family and staff involved in the organization and funding of these camps, but some of his teammates have joined in to support the foundation's efforts. They recently held the 4th annual basketball camp for the inner-city kids of Los Angeles. Children from five years old to fourteen were invited to attend, but nobody had more fun and enjoyment than the "big" basketball kids who were sharing their love of the game.

The camp helps kids to learn basketball basics, and they get to play scrimmage games with some of the best in the business. At camp's end, the children receive awards for their participation and achievements. When asked why Westbrook got involved with the inner-city kids in some of the most violent communities in the United States, his response was "WHY NOT?"

Your guess is as good as ours about what will be Russell Westbrook's next success step, but one thing we know. He'll be taking it with all the wild abandon and enthusiasm that he shows on the basketball court. You can take it to the bank that everyone involved with his next success will have a very good time, and learn to let themselves go the Westbrook way.

Although he has avoided questions about his relationship with Durant since his departure, most of his fans can appreciate his feelings. There's no pretense to smooth them over with circular responses as to his disappointment that Durant left the team, and so his coaches, teammates, and loyal fans share in his displeasure. The wounds are still a bit raw, but Westbrook has a capacity to recover quickly and take out his frustrations by putting up high numbers on the boards.

Since he was a kid, Westbrook's been fighting his battles by playing basketball, and the loss of his teammate doesn't change that. He has more reason than ever to set everybody's mind at rest about what's going to happen to the Thunder with the breakup of their most famous twosome. What's going to happen? Westbrook's going to continue to score those triple-doubles and get career-high rebounds and assists. He's going to be verbal and hot-tempered, and he's going to continue to take Durant's loss personally. Through it all, he's going to do whatever it takes to win.

If Westbrook were to make a move from the Thunder in the next few years, where might he go? It's difficult to guess what motivates trades in the NBA. Just about the time you believe you know what's happening, up pops the unexpected. However, our guess is that this time location might win over compensation. If Westbrook has anything to say about it, perhaps he'll return to his roots in Los Angeles. That means, either the Clippers or the Lakers. The Lakers have the name, but the Clippers might one-up them with the need. For Westbrook, there's nothing like being needed, and that might win over the prestige of going with a team like the Lakers. This of course, is all speculation.

Furthermore, most of the time players aren't considered much when it comes to making a move—even those like Westbrook who have given their all for the team. Not to say he wasn't well compensated, but when you play with your heart, you sometimes leave your heart with the team you left. No matter where Westbrook plays, his fans will be sure to give him all the admiration and respect they've shown him throughout the years. Not because he demands it, but because he deserves it.

One wonders whether announcing or coaching would be in the cards for Westbrook, and rightfully so. What he could teach to other young rookies might lift the game to a whole new level. His experience with the foundation's basketball camps has given him some background, and his team leadership provides him with a taste of what to expect from a new career in coaching. With Westbrook's positive personality and natural leadership skills, coaching makes sense.

One of Westbrook's next successful endeavors that are a given is that he'll make an amazing father. He's had excellent teachers in Russell Sr. and his mother, Shannon Horton. They gave him the foundations of a great life, and he's sure to pass on all the love and caring that his parents provided.

You probably wonder why we're talking about future success steps with a man like Westbrook—a man who has the world by the tail. After all, anybody with that much money would have to be happy, right? Well, if Westbrook could tell it, I'm sure he'd say that although money makes life easier, it doesn't necessarily guarantee happiness. Money doesn't mean success; it sometimes brings with it disillusionment and depression.

Westbrook's measurement of success is family, friends, and living life as he chooses. He's more than willing to do the work and takes responsibility for his setbacks. You cannot put a value on the freedoms he has experienced because he had a talent that he was willing to sacrifice and sweat to build into a career empire. Many people will casually say, "I would do anything to be able to play like Westbrook," but would you?

Would you practice your jump shot for hours alone in a gym while your friends went out with their girlfriends? Would you leave your family for days at a time while you went on the road, staying at a different hotel night after night? Would you put your safety on the line to make a point that might or might not win the game for your team? Would you get yelled at by coaches and criticized by fans and press because you sometimes showed too much passion for the game? Okay, perhaps you would if you were getting paid tens of millions of dollars playing in front of millions of basketball fans who loved you, right? But, what about if you were a lightweight fifteen-year-old whose stature and status in life almost guaranteed that the NBA was going to be outside your circle? Could you maintain the intensity?

Westbrook is a basketball gladiator, a court king, but he's worked hard to earn his position. He's battled personal losses, injuries, disappointments, and made sacrifices that many of us would be unwilling or unable to make. All this for the love of the game.

That's his first and last success step as he walks on and off the court as a role model and hero to millions of kids across the country who share his passion for basketball and his need to excel. His legend as a player is the success that will live forever in the annals of the most elite players in the world. Look there, and you'll find Russell Westbrook III's name written as one of the most remarkable NBA stars ever to hit the courts.

Conclusion

Thanks again for taking the time to read this book, I hope you found it to be insightful.

You should now have a good understanding of Russell Westbrook's life, career, and values. What exactly is next for this superstar, we don't know. But you can be sure that it will be exciting to watch!

If you enjoyed this book, please take the time to leave me a review on Amazon – it helps me to continue producing high quality books!

Made in the USA
Lexington, KY
02 March 2018